Endorse

As a Christian, the celebration of the Advent season is always a highlight for the birth of our Savior. As I read the title, *The Scandal of Christmas*, my curiosity was heightened to know more about the four unlikely figures of the Christmas story. Bill's writing about people's faithfulness to serve, living as ordinary people in an extraordinary event, and seeing the incarnate Jesus' entry into humanity fed my curiosity beyond expectations. The prayers following each character in the story were uplifting and a good reminder of God's perfect love for us. We have the best news to share with others—the gospel of Jesus Christ to those who have never heard. The true Christmas story is still relevant for our world.

—Mike Dragon, Global Director of Every Community for Christ, One Mission Society, Greenwood, Indiana

Fascinating and insightful are two words that describe this book. The characters in the nativity story are described so uniquely that it draws you in and makes them come alive. Dr. Coker reminds us that these were real, ordinary people, just like us. They struggled with doubts, disappointments, shame, and being in the shadows. Yet because of their faith and obedience, they carried out the extraordinary. Their actions still affect our world today. God calls us to the same life of faith and obedience. The question one must ask after reading this book is: Are we willing to be an ordinary Christian to serve a desperately needy world? That is something you will ponder as you read about each character in *The Scandal of Christmas*.

—Patricia D. Dragon, Ministry Trainer,
Every Community for Christ, One Mission Society,
Greenwood, Indiana

The Scandal of Christmas is the scandal of the intensely personal doctrine of the Incarnation. The Son of God left the "sacred precincts of the Holy Place" and chose to live "ingloriously in the midst of the profane." The word ordinary takes center stage in these wonderful pages and paradoxically points us to a most extra-ordinary Savior. The cries of the seemingly ordinary babe of Bethlehem shatters any notion that God is uninterested, or uninvolved, in the lives of peasants, common laborers, forgotten people—and sinners like you and me—who appear to live "only in the shadows of history." With a shepherd's heart, Dr. Bill Coker warmly and magnificently draws our hearts and wills closer to the One who uses the ordinary to bring about His divine purposes.

—Mike Spencer, President, Project LifeVoice,
Celina, Ohio

Ah, how good it is to be sitting under the teaching of Dr. Coker once again! As I read this, I recognized many of his points that have become part of my "knowledge bank" that I draw on for daily living. I had forgotten that it was his teaching on the "irreverence of Jesus" that had helped me to see and experience "all of life as sacred when we live to the praise of His glory." His sermons and prayers are so rich with ideas, that I am very grateful for another chance to harvest them for more insights to live by. And now that they are in print, I will be able to return again and again to add to and refresh my principles of living. May they help others, as they have helped me, to begin to "live a life worthy of the Lord [by] ... growing in the knowledge of God" (Colossians 1:10).

—**Sarah Yoder, PhD, Brazil, Indiana,**
member of World Gospel Church

At Christmas time each year, we hear many sermons about characters related to the birth of Jesus. One unique sermon Dr. Bill Coker preached sincerely spoke to my heart and has remained there for years—Joseph, the man in the shadows. Joseph was a true example in many ways of our steadfast faith in Jesus' divine birth. It is a chapter not to miss!

—**Mary Jo Morrow, Retired Teacher,**
Wilmore, Kentucky

The Scandal of Christmas, although short, touched the core of Christianity. Dr. Coker genuinely unfolded the birth of Jesus by simply looking at four figures: Zechariah, Joseph, Mary, and Jesus himself. From a small town OB/GYN who has delivered over ten thousand babies into this world, I humbly enjoyed Dr. Coker's Advent book.

—**Vannara Sakbun, MD/PhD/FACOG,**
Terre Haute, Indiana

THE SCANDAL OF CHRISTMAS

Advent Reflections on Four Unlikely Figures

Dr. William B. Coker, Sr.

with Ann L. Coker, editor

Foreword by Rev. Dr. William B. Coker, Jr.

Cover design by Dave O'Connell and Robin Black
Illustrations by Dave O'Connell
Author photo used with permission by Scott Kokoska

EABooks Publishing
www.eabookspublishing.com

The Scandal of Christmas
by Dr. William B. Coker, Sr.
with Ann L. Coker, editor

ISBN: 978-1-953114-31-0
LCCN: 2021920540

To
our children,
God's greatest gifts to us:
Bill Coker, Jr.
John Coker
Becky Gearhart
Tom Coker

TABLE OF CONTENTS

Foreword by Rev. Dr. William B. Coker, Jr............... xi

Preface by Ann L. Coker xiii

Zechariah: the faithful man God remembered –
    Luke 1:5–23 1

Joseph: the ordinary man in the shadows –
    Matthew 1:18–25 17

Mary: the peasant girl behind the Creed –
    Luke 1:26–56... 31

Jesus: the irreverent Word made flesh –
    John 1:1–18 51

Endnotes.. 69

Acknowledgements.. 73

About the Author 75

FOREWORD

Those who have known my father, Bill Coker, as their pastor or professor or read his books, *Words of Endearment: The Ten Commandments as a Revelation of God's Love* or *Prayers for the People from the Heart of a Pastor,* will attest to the richness of his vocabulary in English and biblical languages. His command of the dictionary often stretches our understanding and challenges us to the depth of word meanings. We may regard a scandal initially as that which discredits a person, institution, or idea; however, it also may be an intentional stone of offense, a rock of stumbling, a trap or snare necessary to our understanding, fear, and acceptance in the path of faith (Isaiah 8:13–15). Isaiah prophesized the sending of a stone, a precious cornerstone (Isaiah 28:16), which Peter later identified as Jesus Christ that was also a stone of stumbling and rock of offense because He was rejected (1 Peter 2:4–9).

God's scandalous activity through four familiar, yet unlikely, individuals are presented here in four sermons of an Advent series. They challenge us to think deeper and experience anew what it means to believe in and live in relationship to God. Zechariah's patient faithfulness, Joseph's extraordinary ordinariness, Mary's agonizing blessedness, and the irreverent reality of God's incarnation in Jesus challenges us to see that God is at work within our lives, too. These messages "preach Christ [born, crucified, resurrected, ascended, and returning], a stumbling block to [many] . . . but to those whom God has called . . . Christ the power of God and the wisdom of God" (1 Corinthians 1:23–24). Perhaps it is scandalous or irreverent to suggest it, but devout reflection on these chapters during the Advent season will transform your Christmas holiday into holy, joyous, life-changing good news.

I invite you, as my father has, to read, consider, and discover God's plan for you.

—**William B. Coker, Jr., D.Min.† Pastor, Powhatan Point Church of the Nazarene**

PREFACE

"Come, Thou long-expected Jesus . . . Born a child and yet a king" (Charles Wesley).[1]

The four Sundays leading up to Christmas Eve are commonly called Advent. The Christian liturgical calendar begins with Advent and ends with All Saints' Day.

For most families, preparations for Christmas start before or after Thanksgiving Day. Who will come to visit? What is on each child's wish list? Where do we display the nativity set? What will be served for the big meal? Somewhere in all that, perhaps we will light candles on an Advent wreath and attend a Christmas Eve service.

For pastors, or at least the one I know well (my husband, Bill Coker), the decision about an Advent series of messages had to be planned long before Thanksgiving. It was a challenge to infuse new life into passages that had become very familiar both to him and the parishioners. What else can be said after preaching on Christmas for so many years? Yet we all know Scripture is inexhaustible in its readings and impact.

One year Bill chose to preach a series on four biblical personalities and their part in the Christmas story we hold dear. He titled the series: "The Irreverence of the Incarnation." The messages from the Gospels included Zechariah, Joseph, Mary, and Jesus. The sermon that held our interest the most emphasized the least likely character—Joseph, whom Bill referred to as "the man in the shadows."

All these stories bring us closer to the truth of the gospel. Read and reflect.

—**Ann L. Coker**

ZECHARIAH

ZECHARIAH
the faithful man God remembered

I n the time of Herod king of Judea there was a
priest named Zechariah, who belonged to the
priestly division of Abijah; his wife Elizabeth
was also a descendant of Aaron. Both of them were
righteous in the sight of God, observing all the Lord's
commands and decrees blamelessly. But they were
childless because Elizabeth was not able to conceive,
and they were both very old.

Once when Zechariah's division was on duty and
he was serving as priest before God, he was chosen
by lot, according to the custom of the priesthood, to
go into the temple of the Lord and burn incense. And
when the time for the burning of incense came, all the
assembled worshipers were praying outside.

Then an angel of the Lord appeared to him, stand-
ing at the right side of the altar of incense. When
Zechariah saw him, he was startled and was gripped
with fear. But the angel said to him: "Do not be afraid,
Zechariah; your prayer has been heard. Your wife
Elizabeth will bear you a son, and you are to call him
John. He will be a joy and delight to you, and many
will rejoice because of his birth, for he will be great in

the sight of the Lord. He is never to take wine or other fermented drink, and he will be filled with the Holy Spirit even before he is born. He will bring back many of the people of Israel to the Lord their God. And he will go on before the Lord, in the spirit and power of Elijah, to turn the hearts of the parents to their children and the disobedient to the wisdom of the righteous—to make ready a people prepared for the Lord."

Zechariah asked the angel, "How can I be sure of this? I am an old man and my wife is well along in years."

The angel said to him, "I am Gabriel. I stand in the presence of God, and I have been sent to speak to you and to tell you this good news. And now you will be silent and not able to speak until the day this happens, because you did not believe my words, which will come true at their appointed time."

Meanwhile, the people were waiting for Zechariah and wondering why he stayed so

long in the temple. When he came out, he could not speak to them. They realized he had seen a vision in the temple, for he kept making signs to them but remained unable to speak.

When his time of service was completed, he returned home. —Luke 1:5–23

We can only imagine the thoughts that crowded his mind. The aged priest Zechariah entered the Temple to offer incense at the hour of worship. God had been silent for hundreds of years—no prophet, no new revelation of divine purpose, no indication of ancient promises soon to be fulfilled. Zechariah knew the Scriptures, all the accounts of God's dealings with His people in the ages past. He had no reason to expect anything different. It was another ordinary day.

On the other hand, this was a special day. With so many priests they divided into twenty-four courses, each course serving in the Temple only two weeks per year. The privilege of offering up the incense came only once in a lifetime to a priest, and after waiting all those years, the lot had fallen to Zechariah. He, no doubt, was deeply moved to participate in this most hallowed moment in worship. The people in the outer court lifted their prayers as he approached the altar. The incense symbolized their acknowledgement of God and their consecration to Him. This was a spiritually exhilarating moment.

Yet all of his spiritual expectation could not have prepared Zechariah for what happened next. An angel of the Lord appeared, and the Bible says Zechariah was confounded, thrown into disorder. Fear fell on him. We can understand his reaction. The presence of an angelic visitor under any circumstance would be disconcerting. And how could anyone respond but with a sense of awe?

Of course, today we are at a distinct advantage. We possess the New Testament and 2000 years of Church history to fill us in on what was happening. The "fullness of time" had come. God was about to launch the grand scheme of world redemption; and it would begin with this aged priest Zechariah and his wife Elizabeth. They would have a son and name him John. He would be the forerunner of the Messiah.

However, we also have a disadvantage. It is difficult for us to grasp the personal dimension caught up in the angel's message: "Do not be afraid, Zechariah; your prayer has been heard" (Luke 1:13).

"What prayer?" "Why, your prayer for a son." "For a son? That was years ago when my wife and I were young. I am an old man, and my wife is well beyond childbearing age."

It is easy to read the biblical account and lose the human dimension. Behind Zechariah's response lie the futility and frustration of those years of emptiness. It wasn't simply that they had wanted children and could have none. There was the reproach dumped on Elizabeth for being barren. In those days, women were for having babies and when she didn't, she was even less than a woman, a person whom other women could look down on. You sense that in what followed:

> When his time of service was completed, [Zechariah] returned home. After this his wife Elizabeth became pregnant and for five months remained in seclusion.

"The Lord has done this for me," she said, "In these days he has shown his favor and taken away my disgrace among the people" (Luke 1:23–25).

Even Zechariah's Temple service was a period of waiting. For years, when his course was on duty, the lot had fallen to others to burn incense at the altar before the Holy of Holies. How many times had the lot fallen to other priests, even much younger ones? And still he waited. Perhaps he had already begun to think this privilege was likely never to be his.

"Your prayer has been heard" (v. 13). Small wonder Zechariah had trouble believing. If you are the least bit tempted to feel spiritually superior to the old priest, forget it! Those years of futile waiting would not have been borne any more graciously by any of us.

In fact, it's precisely here we gain a marvelous insight into Zechariah and Elizabeth, and we can appreciate why God chose them to be the parents of the forerunner of the Son of God. They had never allowed personal disappointments to divert them from spiritual responsibilities: "Both of them were righteous in the sight of God, observing all the Lord's commands and decrees blamelessly" (v. 6). In spite of all those frustrations, feelings that life had passed them by, none of that interfered with their relationship with God. They walked in righteousness. And after the many years of waiting for the lot to fall on him to offer the incense before God, on that day Zechariah was there. Faithfully there!

It cannot be coincidence that the one whom God would choose to initiate His redemptive activities was named Zechariah. For a Jew, that name had significance. His name means "Yahweh has remembered." You will recall that Yahweh or Jehovah is God's covenant name, the name given to the Israelites by Moses as God's personal name: "I Am." "I Am has remembered."

The Christmas story is the story of God's remembering—and not simply recalling, but acting on behalf of His people to fulfill His purposes. Through centuries past God had remembered and met the needs of His people. How appropriate for the story to begin with "Yahweh has remembered." Zechariah waited in the Temple remembering Yahweh, offering his prayers and the prayers of the people.

God has remembered His people

Countless times throughout the centuries, God had promised His help. Even when His people were wallowing in their sins, God remembered His promise. When Jerusalem was about to be destroyed by the invading Babylonians, God's prophet, Jeremiah, proclaimed a new covenant:

"The days are coming," declared the LORD, "when I will raise up for David a righteous Branch, a King who will reign wisely and do what is just and right in the land. In his days Judah will be saved and Israel will live in safety. This is the name by which he will be called: The LORD Our Righteous Savior" (Jeremiah 23:5–6).

Note what Zechariah said when John was born:

"Praise be to the Lord, the God of Israel, because he has come to his people and redeemed them. He has raised up a horn of salvation for us in the house of his servant David (as he said through his holy prophets of long ago), salvation from our enemies and from the hand of all who hate us—to show mercy to our ancestors and to remember his holy covenant, the oath he swore to our father Abraham" (Luke 1:68–73).

God has remembered His people, but we see more.

God has remembered His world

Luke has such a global perspective in his account. Scholars have referred to Matthew as "the Jewish gospel," and in many ways it may be so. But that cannot be said of Luke. Here we find Zechariah saying of his son John:

> And you, my child, will be called a prophet of the Most High; for you will go on before the Lord to prepare the way for him, to give his people the knowledge of salvation through the forgiveness of their sins, because of the tender mercy of our God, by which the rising sun will come to us from heaven to shine on those living in darkness and in the shadow of death, to guide our feet into the path of peace (Luke 1:76–79).

Later the angels sang to the shepherds: "'Glory to God in the highest heaven, and on earth peace to those on whom his favor rests'" (Luke 2:14).

After Jesus' birth, Joseph and Mary brought the infant Jesus into the temple. We hear there the devout Simeon say of the Christ child:

> Sovereign Lord, as you have promised, you may now dismiss your servant in peace. For my eyes have seen your salvation, which you have prepared in the sight of all nations: a light for revelation to the Gentiles, and the glory of your people Israel (Luke 2:29–32).

The Christmas story is universal, for older than the Mosaic promise to the people of Israel was the Abrahamic promise to the world: "and all nations on earth will be blessed through him" (Genesis 18:18).

And even earlier than the Abrahamic covenant was the covenant God made with the human race after the tragedy of the Fall. Speaking to the serpent (Satan), God said: "And I will put enmity between you and the woman, and between your offspring and hers; he will crush your head, and you will strike his heel" (Genesis 3:15).

God remembered His People and His world, but I want you to hear about an old priest and his barren wife.

God remembered an old couple's faithfulness
How easy it is in the grand scheme of world redemption to write with such bold strokes that we lose sight of the small things, the people involved. It is indeed with a wide brush and broad strokes we paint the glory of Christmas: "God so loved the world" (John 3:16). God has remembered His people, Israel, and sent the day star from on high to shine its brilliant light of salvation. All of that is true.

But now in the fine print we have the story of an old priest and his wife, who faithfully kept the law of God, although their hearts had been hurt by childlessness, and their faith had borne the agony of unanswered prayers for years. God remembered Zechariah and Elizabeth, and that is an integral part of the story of Christmas.

But what do we take from the story in relation to our present lives? Is Christmas only a marvelous story to be told each year—like watching *The Miracle on 34th Street* for the 34th time? Let me suggest some pertinent personal truths. These spoke to me, and I trust they speak to you.

God's answers to prayer are not always as we may wish or understand. We see that with the aged priest. I'm confident that Zechariah went to his temple duty more than once with a prayer on his heart for a child. I'm sure he didn't understand why God did not respond.

His story teaches us today that it's much easier to be Christian when neatly provided responses to our human predicaments and agonies come quickly after the "Amen" of our prayers. We have real difficulty with the idea that God's answer could be other than we think or desire.

One reason that Reverend Ike[2] of the airwaves was successful is people want a god who wants what they want. People will stand in line for an easy kind of faith. The problem is that such a god is not the God of the Bible—Yahweh, Jehovah God. It takes a couple like Zechariah and Elizabeth to teach us about faithfulness.

Another lesson: God sometimes permits our suffering for His glory. We may take this first chapter of Luke and say it's wonderful that God gave this aged couple the privilege of being the parents of the forerunner to the Messiah. But we forget one thing. God allowed Zechariah and Elizabeth to go through those years of barrenness, bearing the reproach of the people and the silence of heaven, because He had something else in mind.

Jesus did the same in the case of Lazarus. After He knew of His friend's illness, Jesus tarried. He said, "This sickness will not end in death. No, it is for God's glory so that God's Son may be glorified through it" (John 11:4). We've forgotten another part of the story. God allowed Mary and Martha to go through the death of their brother. In particular, they also went through the anguish, sorrow, and hurt caused by Jesus' absence—because He had something else in mind.

It's that "something else" that's hard to accept. How could anything be better than what I can plainly see? Sometimes God permits our suffering for His glory. And to accept suffering for His glory is difficult, apart from a full surrender to His will.

A third observation: God always honors faithfulness. Zechariah continued his faithful obedience, even though his answer or blessing did not come.

John Bright wrote the following in his book, *The Kingdom of God*:

The pagan, be he ancient or modern, will understand it as the function of religion to repay him in tangible terms for his worship. He will desire this cozy understanding with his god; that his prayers will return him protection, his dollars more dollars. Nor will he be likely to stick with a religion that does not do this.[3]

Where there is commitment without expectation, God's faithfulness will be manifested.

Fourth, God always has a purpose. God was at work for good for Zechariah and Elizabeth. They would not have changed the blessing they got for all the children they would have had. And if we will accept it, God is at work in our lives for good—in ways far more wonderful than we can imagine.

The story of Christmas begins with a wonderful announcement to an elderly couple: they would be parents of the forerunner of the Messiah. In some ways it's a simple story of ordinary, yet faithful people. And we see personal dimensions that relate to us today. We also have questions about unanswered prayers.

Under it all is the message of Advent. God has remembered, and God still remembers. He remembers you; He remembers us; He remembers His world. He has not forgotten.

Prayer

Our heavenly Father, as we come to offer our prayers before You, we confess we do not know how to pray. We find all too often that our prayers are but an extension of our desires and reflect more interest in ourselves than in You. We have our own personal agendas, ambitions, and aims; and when we pray, we find ourselves asking You to do what we want.

Even this most sacred season of the year, the celebration of the coming of Your Son into our world, has become so oriented to us that our giving and getting is the central focus of our activities. We enjoy these pleasures of Christmas, and we do not ask they be taken away from us; but at least for those of us who call ourselves by Your name, there should be a rediscovery of the holiness of Christmas and a renewed determination to put Christ in the center of our celebrations.

Father God, we thank You for this Christmas season. What a joyous time to be alive; to remember You so loved the world that You gave us Your Son Jesus Christ. It all began with a manger in Bethlehem. It began with ordinary folks pursuing their ordinary routines of life, sometimes with great anguish and deep hurt. Sometimes it was with a bit of wistfulness as they thought of what might have been.

In the midst of all that, what shines out so beautifully is the simple truth: God remembers.

You sent John to an elderly couple as Your messenger to prepare the way for the Messiah.

Grant during this Advent season that we may be ready for Your way—by turning to You and opening our hearts, by hearing Your word and receiving its truth, by walking in faithful obedience, and by giving You full reign in our lives.

You, Lord, remember us. Even in our most difficult circumstances we see evidences of Your bountiful blessings. Help us to learn from these ordinary people that we too can have faith to believe we are blessed even when our lives are less than what we want.

In Christ's dear name we pray. Amen.

JOSEPH

JOSEPH

the ordinary man in the shadows

*T*his is how the birth of Jesus the Messiah came about: His mother Mary was pledged to be married to Joseph, but before they came together, she was found to be pregnant through the Holy Spirit. Because Joseph her husband was faithful to the law and yet did not want to expose her to public disgrace, he had in mind to divorce her quietly.

But after he had considered this, an angel of the Lord appeared to him in a dream and said, "Joseph son of David, do not be afraid to take Mary home as your wife, because what is conceived in her is from the Holy Spirit. She will give birth to a son, and you are to give him the name Jesus, because he will save his people from their sins."

All this took place to fulfill what the Lord had said through the prophet: "The virgin will conceive and give birth to a son, and they will call him Immanuel" (which means "God with us").

When Joseph woke up, he did what the angel of the Lord had commanded him and took Mary home as his wife. But he did not consummate their marriage until *she gave birth to a son. And he gave him the name Jesus.* —Matthew 1:18–25

Most Saturdays a group of boys met to play sandlot ball in my neighborhood. Self-appointed captains chose team members. Looking each captain in the eyes, I waited anxiously to hear my name called. I didn't care which team, only to be chosen. Not drafted on the first or second round, I shuffled my feet in the dirt, still hopeful. Being chosen last did not set well with anyone. Finally, one captain called my name and I moved beside the other chosen until we had a full team.

No one likes to be left out. Regardless of the occasion, to be slighted wounds our pride and sometimes threatens our sense of self-worth. Most of us can easily recall a time when we were passed over, disregarded, or simply forgotten.

The Christmas story has such a person. The Star of Bethlehem cast its brilliance on the Virgin Mary and her infant Son Jesus, but Joseph stands back in the shadows. There isn't a carol written about him; although the shepherds, the magi, and even "Good King Wenceslas" have been immortalized in song. No one sings to honor Joseph. The Gospel of Mark does not mention Joseph's name; John has only two indirect references to him; Luke acknowledges his presence but little more. Only Matthew gives any insight into the man, and that is limited.

Of course, someone will remind us that our belief in the Virgin Birth makes any central role for Joseph unnecessary. In fact, the Roman Catholic Church believes in the perpetual virginity of Mary, that Joseph and Mary never lived as husband and wife, pushing him even further back into the shadows. At the same time, it has to be observed that the Roman Church has canonized Joseph, giving him more prominence than he normally receives in Protestant circles.

Joseph, ignored then and now

Whatever the view, Joseph is a minor character in the Christmas story and is unlikely to be voted an Oscar for "best supporting role." Joseph is simply ignored. Strange as it may seem, it is this fact that calls our attention to Joseph as we think of the human dimensions of the Christmas event. As we listen to the story again, we can identify with how human Joseph is.

The first fact we discover about Joseph was not commendatory in first century Palestine: he was from Nazareth. Later, the disciple Nathanael would exclaim, "Nazareth! Can anything good come from there?" (John 1:46).

The announcement of the forerunner to the Messiah had been made in the Temple to the priest Zechariah, and that no doubt was as it should have been. After all, the Temple was the focal point of Jewish worship. Even though the Pharisees would have preferred someone other than a priest,[4] the Temple at the time of sacrifice was a nice touch.

For any pious Jew in Jerusalem, the Christmas account regressed from the sublime to the ridiculous. The Messiah would be born into an unlettered family in Galilee, in the town of Nazareth! Inconceivable! A humble laborer, whose dialect was contemptible, would not have been approved by the religious leaders.Joseph had no redeeming characteristics, religiously or intellectually, to have recommended him as a religious elite of his day. That God should have chosen him for any role in the coming of the Messiah, at least for a good Jerusalem Jew, bordered on being obscene.

We all know the story. The angel Gabriel appeared to Mary, announced her pregnancy, and told her the child to be born was the Messiah. At the time, Mary was betrothed to Joseph, and although betrothal was as binding as marriage in Jewish culture, their custom dictated a year's interval before the actual marriage took place. Following the angelic announcement, Mary went to the home of her kinspeople, the aged Zechariah and Elizabeth, and spent three months there.

We can understand why Mary would want to get away, and why she had not yet told Joseph of the angel and the message about the Messiah. She returned to Nazareth three months later—three months pregnant. We can imagine what a jarring shock this must have been to her intended. All of his hopes, all of his plans, were out the window.

Matthew wrote that Joseph "was faithful to the law" (1:19), which was to say, he was a just man. That makes Joseph's story more difficult. Mary's supposed unfaithfulness was not only a repudiation of her love for Joseph, but also a rejection of the Law of God. No matter how much he loved her, he could not marry her now.

To top it all off, she had told him an incredible story. An angel had appeared and told her the Spirit of God would cause her to conceive—without a man involved. Joseph decided he would not take her to court and divorce her. The Law provided another way; he would do it privately before two witnesses. Regardless of what she had done, he would not shame her.

Joseph, the good man

Here we begin to see the personal qualities in Joseph. His unwillingness to put further shame on Mary was more than the action of a nice guy. It was indicative of the sensitivity, which marked the man. Mary would already be shamed: the divorce, the obvious pregnancy, the so-called illegitimate child. He had no intention to add abuse to shame. Regardless of what she had done, he did not need or want to get even.

The part about the angel? The Bible doesn't tell us how Joseph handled that aspect of Mary's story.

It would have been difficult for him to process. As much as it would for any of us! One might conjecture this was part of Joseph's reason for a private divorce: he felt sorry for Mary. She believed this story of the angel's visitation. However, in no way do we find in Joseph a scoffing attitude. Whatever Joseph may or may not have understood, he would not ridicule his betrothed. He would simply put her away quietly.

More must be noted. Joseph was evidently a spiritually sensitive man, for the dominant feature of Matthew's portrait is that on four occasions God spoke to Joseph through dreams, giving instruction or warning. A person only nominally religious, or insincere in his devotion to God, could hardly have been that sensitive to the Lord. We can only wonder whether the infrequency with which we today sense God speaking could be the problem of the transmitter or the receiver. It's noteworthy that those who have been most used of God have been those who have been most sensitive to His speaking. Joseph received the messages from his dreams, understood, and acted upon the communication.

One other observation about Joseph's qualities: he was flawless in his obedience to God's will. It reads casually. The humble dimension is found several times: in the reversal of Joseph's decision to divorce Mary; in the decision to leave Bethlehem to go to Egypt; in the decision to return to Palestine; and in the decision to return to Nazareth. These cannot be glossed over. These were life-changing decisions. These were faith decisions. These were risky decisions. Only because we know the story well, do we pass over those points easily.

God chose Mary to be the mother of the Messiah. But I cannot doubt Joseph's character was part of God's choice for the human family within which the Word would become flesh. Joseph was to be the legitimizer of Christ's birth, the earthly father and protector of God's Son. We do a disservice to our Lord's humanity to whitewash these findings by reference to Christ's divinity.

Joseph was without question a good man and a significant part of the Christmas story. Here's the point: for all of that, he is still in the shadows. No prominence, no recognition, and little mention of Joseph in Scripture and Church history. Why then a sermon about Joseph? Because we can readily identify with Joseph, and because important lessons are to be learned from him.

Lessons from Joseph

Most of us dream great dreams as young people. We envision ourselves becoming famous or making a significant contribution to history. This is as it should be. As we reach middle age and begin the descent on the further side, we realize we will not be another Mozart or Einstein or Pasteur or Martin Luther King or Hudson Taylor. We will live only in the shadows of history and be one of the forgotten.

Noted medical professionals tell us this is the trigger for many midlife crises, especially among males. I believe one source is parent-child tension, because we try to dream the impossible dream through our children. We seek to accomplish through them what we failed to reach ourselves. This is not to suggest what ought to be abandoned is parental encouragement to utilize our children's gifts and strive for their potential. We cannot, however, allow our frustrated ambitions and desire for recognition be placed as a burden on our children.

For those of us who live in the shadows, Joseph provides several good lessons.

First, regardless of our role, God has called us to a life of faith and obedience. Often we hear the exhortation, "Be faithful in the little things, and God will give you great things." This is not true encouragement. While there is little doubt God will not trust great causes to people who are unfaithful in small matters, it is also not true that obedience is always rewarded with great opportunities.

God used Joseph for a significant task, to be the earthly parent of the Christ child. Joseph was an ordinary man, who lived an ordinary peasant existence in the tiny village of Nazareth, doing the ordinary work of a builder. God used his ordinariness as his contribution to the redemption of the world.

I am firmly convinced this is the way God works most often. The secret for a great movement of the Spirit lies not in the emergence of a new great religious figure, but in the faithful obedience of ordinary people like ourselves.

Oswald Chambers has a line that's apropos:

It is inbred in us that we have to do exceptional things for God: but we have not. We have to be exceptional in the ordinary things, to be holy in mean streets, among mean people, and this is not learned in five minutes.[5]

That's the secret of a dynamic church. Ordinary people who pray, ordinary people who are open to being filled with God's Spirit, ordinary people who share their simple faith, ordinary people with ordinary means who tithe for the sake of the Kingdom of God. These are people being exceptional in the ordinary. God is looking for ordinary people to be ordinary Christians serving a desperately needy world.

A second lesson from Joseph is found in his willingness to risk his reputation to be obedient to God. We can only wonder what whisperings must have gone on about Joseph and Mary when her pregnancy became obvious. People probably criticized Joseph, and the religious community may have openly rebuked him. He knew that would happen. He knew he could never explain what the Lord had done. The Bible is silent, and we can only assume Joseph accepted quietly what people said openly or behind his back. He was that kind of man.

Here is a contrast to what we often find even among professing Christians. "What is it going to cost me?" is more than an idle concern. It's too often the determining factor in obedience. Joseph is a rebuke to every selfish interest that interferes in our obedience to the Lord. It may be about our reputation among our friends or our image among our peers.

As a church, we are always in the process of assessing where we are and where we are going. What is the task to which God has called us? We cannot afford to ask what it will cost to follow God's will into the next decade; we must be willing to be obedient. We cannot retain our freedom unless we are willing to pay the ultimate price.

When we think about the gospel, we remember the price exacted of Joseph and Mary. The Word became flesh in a bloody birth in a cattle stall among the animals, and Jesus came to an untimely death on a bloody cross between two criminals. There is no room for any who want to follow Christ only if it doesn't ask too much of us. Unheralded as he may be, Joseph is a pattern for the life of obedience to which we are all called.

One last lesson I have learned from Joseph. He was a simple man with a simple faith. He was not highly educated and had none of the privileges afforded those from wealthy or noble families. He could not have argued theology with the learned scholars of his day, nor could he have explained the finer points of the Law. He was a common man willing to serve. He received no acclaim and sought no recognition. What he did, he did quietly in service to his Lord.

I have found myself thinking: *I want to be that person who is willing to serve.* And if I could choose the kind of church I would like to serve, it would be a church of Josephs—ordinary people who are willing to serve.

This Christmas, as for every Christmas, the focus of our faith needs to be on the Christ child. But as you envision in your mind's eye the humble realities of the manger setting and the heavenly light shining brilliantly around the infant Jesus, steal a glance over in the shadows. His name is Joseph. He has much to tell us.

Prayer

Jesus, we never cease to marvel that You should have condescended to come and dwell among humanity. It is even more amazing that You should be willing to dwell within us.

We are not many, and we are not exceptional, but we are Your people. We are who we are because of the influence of other lives that have touched ours. We thank You, Lord, for our family and friends who have been good examples for us.

May we be encouraged to think in some way that our lives may be instrumental in changing the course of others' lives. May our commitment to You and the daily practice of that commitment be the guiding light for those among us who grope in darkness.

We pray that we may listen and see in this unheralded man, Joseph, the simple but important truth of his flawless obedience to You and Your word. May we, like Joseph, be willing to follow in obedience to Your will, and to make life-changing decisions that honor You. May this ordinary man of faithfulness move us to a deeper commitment to You.

As we go about our daily responsibilities, cause that inward light of Your presence to shine through the windows of our souls upon our family, our colleagues, and even those whom we meet only causally. Let your grace be greatly observed in our daily lives.

With gratitude, we give You, Lord, our adoration and praise. We love You, Lord. These petitions and thanks we offer in Your name. Amen.

MARY

MARY

the peasant girl behind the Creed

In the sixth month of Elizabeth's pregnancy, God sent the angel Gabriel to Nazareth, a town in Galilee, to a virgin pledged to be married to a man named Joseph, a descendant of David. The virgin's name was Mary. The angel went to her and said, "Greetings, you who are highly favored! The Lord is with you."

Mary was greatly troubled at his words and wondered what kind of greeting this might be. But the angel said to her, "Do not be afraid, Mary; you have found favor with God. You will conceive and give birth to a son, and you are to call him Jesus. He will be great and will be called the Son of the Most High. The Lord God will give him the throne of his father David, and he will reign over Jacob's descendants forever; his kingdom will never end."

"How will this be," Mary asked the angel, "since I am a virgin?"

The angel answered, "The Holy Spirit will come on you, and the power of the Most High will overshadow you. So the holy one to be born will be called the Son of God. Even Elizabeth your relative is going *to have a child in her old age, and she who was said to be unable to conceive is inher sixth month. For no word from God will ever fail."*

"I am the Lord's servant," Mary answered. "May your word to me be fulfilled." Then the angel left her.

At that time Mary got ready and hurried to a town in the hill country of Judea, where she entered Zechariah's home and greeted Elizabeth. When Elizabeth heard Mary's greeting, the baby leaped in her womb, and Elizabeth was filled with the Holy Spirit. In a loud voice she exclaimed: "Blessed are you among women, and blessed is the child you will bear! But why am I so favored, that the mother of my Lord should come to me? As soon as the sound of your greeting reached my ears, the baby in my womb leaped for joy. Blessed is she who has believed that the Lord would fulfill his promises to her!"

And Mary said: "My soul glorifies the Lord and my spirit rejoices in God my Savior, for he has been mindful of the humble state of his servant. From now on all generations will call be blessed, for the Mighty One has done great things for me—holy is his name. His mercy extends to those who fear him, from generation to generation. He has performed mighty deeds with his arm; he has scattered those who are proud in their inmost thoughts. He has brought down rulers from their thrones but has lifted up the humble. He has filled the hungry with good things but has sent the rich away empty. He has helped his servant Israel, remembering to be merciful to Abraham and his descendants forever, just as he promised our ancestors."

Mary stayed with Elizabeth for about three months and then returned home. —Luke 1:26–56

"I believe in God, the Father Almighty, Maker of heaven and earth; and in Jesus Christ, His only Son our Lord, who was conceived by the Holy Spirit, born of the Virgin Mary" (The Apostles' Creed).[6] It reads matter of fact, like a school child reciting a times table or a Latin verb paradigm. Two thousand years after the event, we can mouth the words automatically with little comprehension of or concern for the actual drama that makes the Advent story so exciting.

Within these messages about Advent, we focus our attention on the human dimension of the Christmas story. We seek insight from the lives of those involved and derive lessons for our faith journey. We began with the aged priest Zechariah and his wife Elizabeth, noting their patient persistence and piety. God remembered them and through them remembered His people. Even though Elizabeth was barren and past childbearing age, God gave them a son who was to be the forerunner of the Messiah.

We took Joseph out of the shadows of the Christmas narrative and considered those few details about him, which Matthew's Gospel affords us. We found him to be a model for obedience to

God. We saw how he sought no recognition nor did he receive any acclaim. As a common laborer, he was willing to serve. God used Joseph as the legitimizer of Jesus' birth, the protector of the infant Son of God, and the spiritually sensitive role model for this growing child.

Now we consider Mary, the girl behind the Creed, the one chosen to give birth to the Prince of Peace. Unlike Joseph, she has not faded back into the shadows. She is celebrated for her role in the birth of the Messiah, elevated and esteemed by the Church. When she declared, "From now on all generations will call me blessed" (Luke 1:48), she could not have known how blessed she would be.

For most Protestants, this elevation of Mary by the Roman Catholic Church has dampened our desire to bestow appropriate honor on this Jewish maiden. Such teachings as the doctrine of Immaculate Conception and Assumption of Mary, and such titles as "Queen of Heaven" and "Mother of God," to say nothing of the repetitive praying of the "Hail, Mary," make it difficult for us to retain an objective view of Jesus' mother. When was the last time we heard "Ave Maria" sung in a Protestant worship service?

We do not agree that Mary is an *object* of faith; but we should not overlook her as a *pattern* for faith. Her significant place in the earthly life of our Lord Jesus Christ deserves not only our appreciation, but demands our attention. No higher commendation could be given than to be chosen for such an awesome responsibility of being the mother of the Word incarnate. We want now to peel back the words of the Creed to behold the person. We want to disregard the disputes about her position to consider her example.

As with Joseph, Scripture provides little information about Mary. We know she too was from Nazareth, though there is no mention of her family. Some traditions suggest Mary was an orphan. Whatever the case, Mary was a poor peasant girl whose betrothal to a common builder would have caused little stir among the socially prominent. Other ancient traditions tell us Joseph was a widower, perhaps even a good bit older than Mary. We know by the time Jesus began His public ministry, Joseph was not around; apparently he had already died. If this is true, then our Lord was acquainted with grief in ways beyond His own rejection.

When we portray the nativity, Mary is seen as a mature young woman in her twenties. Actually this is a reflection of our own culture, not of first century Palestine. Mary was probably about fourteen years old when Jesus was born, the typical age for a newly married Jewish girl. Even today in a non-industrialized, non-technological Eastern society, children are ushered into the responsibilities of adult life rather early. We can witness this on the evening news about Afghanistan, Iran, or

Nicaragua, where you see children armed with weapons of war.

Visit from the angel

Mary was only a girl, but old enough to be married. When the angel Gabriel stood before her, you can imagine her reaction to this heavenly intruder. Luke tells us about three stages in Mary's response.

First, the angel's pronouncement of divine favor: "Greetings, you who are highly favored! The Lord is with you." (Luke 1:28). When Luke wrote about the angel's appearance to Zechariah, he was troubled. But Luke used an intensified form of the same word here: Mary was "greatly troubled" (v. 29).

Why should such a messenger come to her? She was not a high priest; she was not a prophet. Indeed, she was not even a man!

Why should the angel call her "highly favored," or as the Latin states, "full of grace"? She knew God's favor was not merited, but why was *she* favored? She was only a poor girl from a poor village in Galilee. Surely God's blessing would be upon those in Jerusalem, those who lived in the shadow of the Holy Temple.

Luke wrote that she "wondered what kind of greeting this might be" (v. 29). We don't know how long Mary stood there in silence before the angel told her not to be afraid, but it was long enough for her to get a discussion going in her mind: "What in the world? What does he mean? Why is he telling me this? What's going to happen?

A second stage: Gabriel told Mary, "You will conceive and give birth to a son, and you are to call him Jesus" (v. 31). Of course, she and Joseph were to be married, but she understood the angel didn't mean eventually. He meant right away! She was confused earlier, but now she was overwhelmed! She was a virgin; she had never been unfaithful, either to God or to Joseph. Besides, if she had, she would not have been favored by God. It was not Mary's lack of faith as in Zechariah's case; it was sheer amazement that made her cry out, "How will this be . . . since I am a virgin?" (v. 34). The Greek would read, "I'm not knowing a man. So how can this be?"

Even more overwhelming than the announcement of her coming pregnancy was what Gabriel said about her son: "He will be great and will be called the Son of the Most High. The Lord God will give him the throne of his father David, and . . . his kingdom will never end" (vv. 32–33).

The heart of every devout Jew beat with anticipation for the time when Messiah would come. There had been claims; false messiahs had led aborted attempts to gain Israel's independence. Mary's son was to be the Messiah. It was incredible! Inconceivable! Impossible! More than any girl could dream.

Mary had gone from being troubled to being astounded. But Gabriel's third announcement was more than *any* human mind could comprehend: "The Holy Spirit will come on you, and the power of the Most High will overshadow you. So the holy one to be born will be called the Son of God." (v. 35).

Let it be firmly established among us that neither in Matthew's nor Luke's account of the Virgin Birth is there any hint of a sexual liaison between God and Mary. *Rosemary's Baby*, a la Hollywood, was supposedly conceived through sexual intercourse with the devil. But concerning Jesus' conception the New Testament scrupulously avoids any suggestion of sex. Matthew used a preposition indicating not agency but source, the Holy Spirit.

The perturbing reality of what the angel told Mary about the son to whom she would give birth is caught up masterfully in the words of Dorothy Sayers in her book *Creed or Chaos?*:

> The Christian faith is the most exciting drama that ever staggered the imagination of man . . . That Jesus Bar-Joseph, the carpenter of Nazareth, was in fact and in truth, and in the most exact and literal sense of the words, the God "by whom all things were made." His body and brain were those of a common man; His personality was the personality of God, so

far as that personality could be expressed in human terms. He was not a kind of demon or fairy pretending to be human; He was in every respect a genuine living man. He was not merely a man so good as to be "like God"—He was God.[7]

Mary, the poor peasant girl of Nazareth could not begin to grasp the enormity of Gabriel's announcement. Her response is beautiful: "I am the Lord's servant. May your word to me be fulfilled" (v. 38). From confusion to amazement to surrender, she offered her willingness for whatever God wanted. She was but a servant, a slave; she wanted nothing other than what her Lord willed.

Then she was alone; the angel left her. Mary would carry this baby, the eternal God incarnate, but she would carry much more. She would alone bear the burden of telling Joseph the incredible account of her encounter with the heavenly messenger. She would bear the whispers of those wagging tongues that spoke judgmentally of her untimely pregnancy. She would bear the hard journey to Bethlehem where she would give birth in less than sanitary conditions. She would bear the flight into Egypt to escape the jealous rage of Herod the Great. She would bear the unanswerable questions of those years of growth when Jesus matured into manhood. She would bear alone the agony and burden caused by those who rejected Jesus' ministry and shamelessly sought His death. As Simeon told her, "a sword will pierce your own soul" (Luke 2:35), so Mary agonized through those seemingly endless hours of Jesus' trial and crucifixion.

Visit with Elizabeth

We can hardly be surprised that after the angel left, Mary went immediately to Elizabeth's home. She no doubt wanted and needed the support she would receive from someone who could identify with what she had experienced. Before she could tell Joseph, she needed time with Elizabeth.

Hope did not disappoint Mary. The confirmation she needed came as soon as she entered the priest's home. There Elizabeth uttered two consolations to Mary.

Immediately Elizabeth confirmed all that had happened. She confirmed the angel's message: "Blessed are you among women, and blessed is the child you will bear!" (Luke 1:42). If Mary had any uncertainty about who her baby was, Elizabeth did not: "Why am I so favored, that the mother of my Lord should come to me?" (v. 43). Since Jews felt that God's name Yahweh was too holy to be spoken, they used the word "Lord" instead. Elizabeth's reference to the "mother of my Lord" was unmistakable. The angel had said Mary's baby would be called the holy Son of God. I want us to feel the human drama, for it was not so automatic as it sounds when we recite the Creed. This was an amazing drama that began the reality of world redemption.

Elizabeth also affirmed Mary personally: "Blessed is she who has believed that the Lord would fulfill his promises to her!" (v. 45). What had taken place was not only a great act of divine love, it was a great act of human faith. This girl, with all of the naiveté of her youth, had dared to believe it would be as the angel had said. A simple faith met an unhesitating surrender.

Elizabeth was the person Mary needed, and for three months they waited together in anxious anticipation. When John was born, Mary knew it was time for her to return home. She must now tell Joseph what God had done.

We pause to consider Mary's poetic response to Elizabeth, the Magnificat, which E. Stanley Jones called "the most revolutionary document in the world."[8] Our concern has been to see something of the human dimension involved in the birth of Christ. Now we must ask, what do we draw from the example of Mary's faith to assist us in our Christian lives? I suggest several lessons.

Lessons on faith

The first practical lesson is rather simple and obvious. It has to do with age. We've already picked up on the interesting difference between Zechariah and Elizabeth on the one hand and Mary on the other. Zechariah and Elizabeth were elderly, approaching the twilight years of life. In our society, they would probably have been retired. Mary, however, was a young girl, no doubt bubbling over with excitement and enthusiasm, anticipating her marriage. The Christmas story incorporates both ends of the age spectrum with a pointed message for us all. God does nothing accidently, so we cannot stumble over His purposes. There is no time in life—too old or too young—when God cannot use us for His purposes.

Many times older persons have excused themselves with the threadbare line, "Well, I'm too old to do much. It's time for younger people to take over." While it is obviously true as we get older, we cannot do certain jobs; it is equally true there are those tasks only *we* can do.

God may never call on us old folks to have babies (hopefully), but we can contribute our wisdom of experience and maturity of faith and prayer, which the young cannot supply.

The great tragedy is we allow age to make us set in our ways. Leaving room for God to do something new, His ways transform others through us.

The flip side is that many young people use their age as a cop-out for bearing responsibility. Mary was a teenage mother, a young teen at that. Other cultures compel their young to mature faster. While that may not be totally acceptable for us, it's a reminder that young people are capable of more than cruising for a good time.

God knows we do not need a church full of somber saints. The gospel does not have a law against fun, and our Lord is not the enemy of good times. But there is a seriousness about life, which our youth must accept and even enjoy. A moral warfare rages in our schools and throughout our society. The church is in need of young people like Mary, who are willing to say, "I am the Lord's servant" (Luke 1:38).

Lest you think I am overstating the case, recall the Old Testament prophet Joel whom Peter quoted on the day of Pentecost:

> In the last days, God says, I will pour out my Spirit on all people. Your sons and daughters will prophesy, your young men will see visions, your old men will dream dreams (Acts 2:17).

It is the will of God for young and old, male and female, to be filled with the Spirit and willing to say, "Thy will be done."

The second lesson: There is a place for simple faith, simply to trust and believe God. The Church has always needed people of great intellect who could plumb the depths of theological wisdom and argue the case for faith for those who do not believe. Peter wrote, "Always be prepared to give an answer to everyone who asks you to give the reason for the hope that you have" (1 Peter 3:15).

It has also been my experience that many in church hesitate to serve, because they are neither learned in theology nor skilled in biblical knowledge. I'm satisfied that what God is looking for in the rank and file of Christian service are those whose simple faith allows Christ to do His will in them. We have too many generals and too few foot soldiers who win the war.

Mary was a teenager, living in a culture that did not grant a large place to women. She could not have handled the ancient scrolls and may not have been able to read if given them. But God took her honesty, her purity, her faith, and her ability to have a baby, and He made her the woman whom the ages have called "blessed." No wonder the early Church venerated her.

If we could make a Christmas list for our churches and request what we need most, we would be tempted to say: "We need more finances to finish this year and begin the new year in the black; and we would like to have sufficient funds to offer many new services to our city." Or: "We could use a new organ (or piano). This old Wurlitzer or Baldwin is about played out. Lord, they're expensive!" Or: "We need more people to broaden our base to carry out the vision of this church. As older warriors are stepping out, we need new ones to step in."

Oh, we could have a list longer than one by Dennis the Menace. But these are only wants.

The *real need* is for people of simple faith, people like Mary.

A third practical lesson has to do with the tension between faith and obedience. Sometimes our discussions heat up as to which is primary. In truth, they are dependent upon each other. Faith is only faith when it acts upon what is believed; and obedience is only obedience when its action is in response to faith in God's will. Mary received the angelic message as God's promise and believed it. Her obedience was itself an act of faith, trusting for the fulfillment of what was spoken to her from the Lord.

All of this is a timely word for us. We will not obey unless we believe God is speaking to us. Until we obey, our faith is weak and ineffective. Most of us know what we need to do. God has spoken to us through His word, through sermons, in our prayer time, through His people. But the powerful movement of the Kingdom of God sits idly by until we begin to obey His will.

We do not need an all-night prayer meeting to flagellate ourselves and plead with God. We have only to say, "I am the Lord's servant. May your word to me be fulfilled" (Luke 1:38).

Take it personally

One last practical word, only a brief observation, but one that is not insignificant. As we seek for personal applications from this Scripture, note that Elizabeth was called to be Elizabeth, and

Mary to be Mary. Not only were their roles different, but also each was important to the other.

Mary's trip to Elizabeth's home and the three months she stayed there were undoubtedly of great significance to the elderly Elizabeth. It brought joy and encouragement in her time of childbearing.

On the other hand, we noted that Elizabeth was a confirmation to Mary of what the angel had said. Her personal affirmation of Mary's faith was probably no small part of Mary's preparation for her return to Nazareth and Joseph, and the wagging tongues of those who could not understand.

The Church has always needed both: the old and the young, men and women. Some will see visions and dare to launch out in faith, and others will affirm and support, making it possible to keep going.

This Christmas, as you set up the manger scene on your coffee table or mantle, and from time to time you stop to admire those little figures that represent the characters in this greatest of all dramas, remember they are *real* people and give thanks. God used those simple people of faith, those who were willing to be available.

Prayer
Grant, Lord Jesus, as we worship You we shall give You access to our lives. Come afresh to us in this season of celebration. As Mary accepted Your

invitation, may we take this opportunity to submit ourselves to Your will.

Lord, we cannot thank You enough for our own invitation to follow You wherever You lead. We thank You for those who have directly inspired us—pastors, missionaries, Sunday school teachers, Christian family and friends.

We thank You, our Father, for this yearly reminder of the birth of Your Son. In a time and place, You caused a virgin girl to conceive and bear a child and to call His name Jesus, Savior. We think about Mary, probably about fourteen years old, accepting the burden of being the mother of the Son of God incarnate.

As we have admired Elizabeth and Mary, help us remember they were ordinary people. We cannot view these people as different from ourselves. Father, these real people have stirred our hearts, because we've found they are so much like us. May we celebrate our age, whether that be young or old, for we can be used by our Savior to proclaim His message of hope and redemption.

O God, challenge our faith to be more than we are. May the peace that passes all understanding keep our hearts and minds in Christ Jesus, in whose name we pray. Amen.

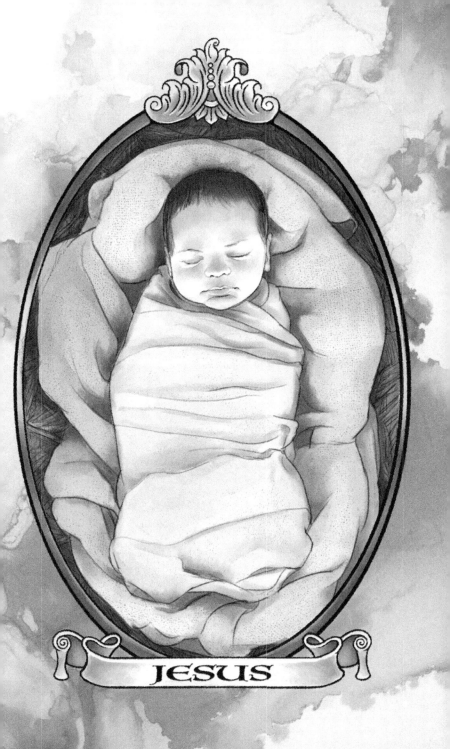

JESUS

JESUS

the irreverent Word made flesh

I n the beginning was the Word, and the Word was with God, and the Word was God. He was with God in the beginning. Through him all things were made; without him nothing was made that has been made. In him was life, and that life was the light of all mankind. The light shines in the darkness, and the darkness has not overcome it.

There was a man sent from God whose name was John. He came as a witness to testify concerning that light, so that through him all might believe. He himself was not the light; he came only as a witness to the light.

The true light that gives light to everyone was coming into the world. He was in the world, and though the world was made through him, the world did not recognize him. He came to that which was his own, but his own did not receive him. Yet to all who did receive him, to those who believed in his name, he gave the right to become children of God—children born not of natural descent, nor of human decision or a husband's will, but born of God.

The Word became flesh and made his dwelling among us. We have seen his glory, the glory of the one and only Son, who came from the Father, full of grace and truth.

(John testified concerning him. He cried out, saying, "This is the one I spoke about when I said, 'He who comes after me has surpassed me because he was before me.'") Out of his fullness we have all received grace in place of grace already given. For the law was given through Moses; grace and truth came through Jesus Christ. No one has ever seen God, but the one and only Son, who is himself God and is in closest relationship with the Father, has made him known. —John 1:1–18

In J. B. Phillips' paraphrase of the New Testament letters, *Introduction to Letters to Young Churches*, C. S. Lewis wrote:

The same divine humility that decreed that God should become a baby at a peasant woman's breast, and later an arrested field preacher in the hands of the Roman police, decreed also that he should be preached in a vulgar, prosaic and unliterary language. If you can stomach the one, you can stomach the other. The Incarnation is in that sense an irreverent doctrine: Christianity, in that sense, an incurably irreverent religion.[9]

To hear the Incarnation referred to as an "irreverent doctrine" comes as a bit of a shock to most of us. But that it should be called *irrelevant* is not at all surprising in a world like ours.

Unbelievers consider the Incarnation and all of Christianity irrelevant because of its unabashed supernaturalism. Of all Christian teaching, none appears to be more out of joint with our contemporary intellectual and secular frame of mind than does the Incarnation—not because it is irrelevant to the modern spiritual need, but because it proposes as fact something which runs counter to the whole naturalistic estimate of man and his situation.

From the announcement of the miraculous conception to the recognition that the Babe of Bethlehem is the Word become flesh, which was in the beginning with God and is God, and from that moment the story is permeated with the sense of the supernatural bursting into the darkness of man's sinful existence like the blazing light of the sun shattering the shades of night. To those who predicate human existence on sheer chance, such supernaturalism is mythological and irrelevant to man come of age.

Some liberal Christians also consider it irrelevant, at least in regard to a divine Incarnation. The charge may be heard in many seminaries and not from a few so-called important pulpits that the Christmas story is out of step with modern man.

The sad story of the last two centuries of Church history reveals the emergence of the same philosophy of unbelief as one finds in the world. It has debunked the supernatural and has seen in the gospels only a human Jesus who was deified by the myths and legends of the Church.

A much more subtle declaration of irrelevancy comes from the other wing of the Church, from those who declare doctrine dull and unnecessary. Christianity for them is a warm fuzzy, whose sum and substance is love. They say, doctrine divides, love unifies. Therefore, let's forget these irrelevant dogmas and just praise Jesus. Of course, as pious as it may sound, Christians must realize this bit of Christmas eggnog is spiked with arsenic. It really spells the death of the Church.

Fundamental to faith

Historically, the Church has declared the Incarnation is foundational to Christian faith, that it is not irrelevant to humanity and our circumstance and need. Scripture is clear: Jesus of Nazareth was indeed and in truth God incarnate, the Word become flesh. The declaration of The Council of Chalcedon in A.D. 451 may read like theological verbiage, but this represents the careful but emphatic conviction of the Church after centuries of struggle over who Jesus Christ really is. It's the question of the deity and humanity of Jesus. The declaration reads in part:

Following the holy fathers, we teach with one voice that the Son of God and our Lord Jesus Christ is to be confessed as one and the same person, that he is perfect in Godhead and perfect in manhood, very God and very Man, a reasonable soul and a human body consisting; consubstantive with the Father as touching his Godhead and consubstantive with us as touching his manhood.[10]

The effort of the Council was to declare that the Word had become flesh. This is hardly irrelevant: it is at one time the most stupendous and incredible event in the history of the human race, and also the most shattering event ever to have taken place.

Incredible? Because it is, as Dorothy Sayers wrote, "The time when God submitted to the conditions He had laid down and became a man like the men He had made, and the men He had made broke Him and killed Him. This is the dogma we find so dull—this terrifying drama of which God is the victim and the hero."[11]

It may be incredible, but this is the announcement of the Christmas story. The Word has indeed become flesh and He is relevant to every person's life.

Devastating? Because the infant cries of the baby Jesus shatter any deistic theism which would profess faith in a transcendent Creator, but not a God who comes down and encounters humanity in the world which He made.

- Those cries of the infant Jesus shatter any naturalistic atheism, which seeks to explain everything within the closed system of natural phenomena.
- Those cries shatter any man-centered or egocentric lifestyle, by which a person seeks to find meaning or happiness in terms of one's own ambitions and desires.
- Those cries shatter any humanistic philosophy, which advocates humanity may redeem itself through a program of progressive self-improvement.
- And those cries shatter any religion that fancies itself to be seeking a god who is afar off, or to bring redemption through its own mysteries and practices.

It is an incredible event. It is a devasting story.

"The Word became flesh and made his dwelling among us. We have seen his glory, the glory of the one and only Son, who came from the Father, full of grace and truth" (John 1:14). William Barclay said, "It might well be held that this is the greatest verse in the whole New Testament."[12]

Whatever you say about Jesus, you cannot say the Babe of Bethlehem is irrelevant! We may not be able to stomach the idea of God becoming "a baby at a peasant woman's breast," and we may set the course of our lives to ignore or reject the manger of Bethlehem, but the Word of God Incarnate remains God's last word to a helplessly floundering humanity.

Irreverent Incarnation

While the Incarnation is not irrelevant, it *is* irreverent. It flies in the face of protocol; it removes God from the sacred precincts of the Holy Place and dumps Him rather ingloriously in the midst of the profane. The Word became flesh. As Charles Wesley exclaimed:

> See the eternal Son of God, A mortal Son of Man;
> Now dwelling in an earthly clod, Whom heaven cannot contain.
> Stand amazed, ye heavens, at this: See the Lord of earth and skies;
> Low humbled to the dust He is, And in a manger lies.[13]

In the early Church, Christians had great difficulty with such irreverence. The Gnostics saw materiality as the lowest state of emanating reality. For them, evil was resident in the physical. To affirm the Son of God as incarnate was improper and unacceptable.

They believed that at the baptism of the man Jesus, the Son of God entered into Him and used

His body. And before the crucifixion of the man Jesus, the Son of God exited Him.

It may be against such teaching that John wrote his first letter:

> That which was from the beginning, which we have heard, which we have seen with our eyes, which we have looked at and our hands have touched—this we proclaim concerning the Word of life . . . which was with the Father and has appeared to us (1 John 1:1, 2).

The same tendency to accept a non-biblical dichotomy between flesh and spirit can be found in some evangelical circles today. It's to see sin only in terms of the material and holiness only in terms of the spiritual. Sanctified living, to some, is a matter of denying the flesh, and the more ascetic one becomes, the more holy.

The pessimism we have about our humanity is expressed in numerous ways:

- We see our human nature as a carnal nature, and one from which we cannot be redeemed until we die.
- We see holiness as impossibility because of the weakness of the flesh. No matter what we do, it is sinful because the flesh has done it.

- We tend to dehumanize the saints of the Bible, viewing them on levels we can never attain. And if we can never be as they were, why try? We have enough frustrations in life without adding another.

That's the shocking irreverence of the Incarnation. It puts the Son of God in the ordinary, everyday garb of one of us. It posits the sacred into the secular, and transforms the secular and makes it sacred.

Does it seem more proper to have a Savior in an angelic robe with a seraphic glow radiating from His face? Isn't that what the Christmas carol states? "Radiant beams from Thy holy face."[14] That's far more worshipful than a Savior who doesn't look any different than any other Jewish baby or a Savior in faded bibs with grease under His fingernails.

Not only is any angelic Jesus more proper for our religious sensitivities, such a Savior is more comfortable for us. As long as I can keep spirituality at a safe distance, I can feel justified in making that an ideal toward which I aspire but which is not within range. But an irreverent Redeemer, one who is a commoner, one who grows up in a blue-collar home and learns a trade and gets his hands dirty, one who puts holy living down on the level of the routine and ordinary, such a Redeemer is terribly inconvenient. The religious leaders in Jerusalem thought that

Jesus could not possibly be the Son of God. They crucified Him.

We find some rather practical implications of this biblical irreverence. It leads to the sanctification of the ordinary. What do I mean by that?

Stop defining sin in terms of humanness and see it for what it is. We are not sinners because we are human beings. Sin is rebellion against the holy God. God's great complaint against us is not that we cannot perform at the level of flawlessness, but that we set our wills against His will to live a life of self-gratification.

Life is sacred

We also need to stop dividing our lives into two unrelated areas, sacred and secular, and see all of life as sacred when we live to the praise of His glory. A.W. Tozer, in his book, *Pursuit of God*, has a marvelous chapter on "The Sacrament of Living." Let me quote:

> Let us think of a Christian believer in whose life the twin wonders of repentance and the new birth have been wrought. He is now living according to the will of God as he understands it from the written word. Of such a one it may be said that every act of his life is or can be as truly sacred as prayer or baptism or the Lord's Supper. To say this is not to bring all acts

down to one level; it is rather to lift every act up into a living kingdom and turn the whole of life into a sacrament.[15]

This is why the Incarnation is irreverent, and Christianity is an incurably irreverent religion. Our religion is not simply what we do in the sanctuary; it is what we do at home, on the job, on the basketball court, on vacation. The activities of the sanctuary have meaning only if our faith is irreverent enough to get our hands dirty with everyday concerns. I wish I could write that indelibly on our hearts.

The sanctification of the ordinary will alter our understanding of prayer. Even though the sentiment expressed in the gospel song, "A little talk with Jesus"—may be too simplistic and misleading, we find the irreverence of our Lord in it. Prayer *can be* "just a little talk with Jesus,"[16] and ought to be so commonplace that any of us can talk with God in our own words. Prayer is a personal approach to an approachable God.

I have viewed the film *Fiddler on the Roof* several times. I love it when Tevye, the main character, looks upward and talks with God. In an honest way, Tevye tells God what's on his mind, yet he knows he's talking with a holy God.

The sanctification of the ordinary dares us to make new applications of old principles to the issues of our day. In spite of all the criticisms leveled at the Pharisees in the New Testament, in contrast to the Sadducees, they at least tried to make the Law applicable to daily life. This often led them to nit picking and legalism, but it was an attempt to make holiness practical. The Law became personal and practical in their lives.

If we would pattern ourselves after the Incarnation of Christ, it should be understood that it will be costly. It will mean a willingness to identify with the needs of others, a willingness to sit "among them," as Ezekiel did (3:15).

What a tremendous illustration of this we find in Hudson, the founder of China Inland Mission. To make the gospel incarnate, he decided to exchange his European clothing for the dress of the Chinese people, and to shave the front part of his head and to grow the hair on the back of his head long enough for a queue. In doing so, he lost the prestige attached to Europeans in China, but he found an open door into the lives of the Chinese people.[17]

Another example was Rees Howells, the Welsh intercessor who discovered one key to intercessory prayer is an identification with those for whom he prayed. Whether it was the widowed child brides of India or the tramps of Wales, Howells was impressed by the Holy Spirit that only as he sought to be "among them" could he intercede effectively. One practice, he would live on one meal every two days. Read his biography,

Rees Howells, Intercessor,[17] and you will find it both inspiring and convicting.

The irreverence of the incarnation will also mean a willingness to be emptied for Christ's sake. St. Paul wrote that when the Word became flesh, "he made himself nothing by taking the very nature of a servant, being made in human likeness" (Philippians 2:7). That was the irreverence of the Incarnation: for the eternal God to accept the limitations of human nature, to become one of us. To follow Christ means a readiness to be emptied. A familiar gospel song states it plainly: "I give up myself, and whatever I know. Now wash me, and I shall be whiter than snow."[18]

In the Roman Empire, before the spread of the gospel, many Gentiles found the ethical monotheism of Judaism attractive. They did not become proselytes, but people knew them as "God-fearers."[19] The reason for not becoming Christian converts was the requirement for males to be circumcised. They would not submit themselves to full identification.

Similarly, many would follow Christ today if it were not for the call to be emptied and to be crucified with Christ. This is the flip side of the Incarnation: as the Son of God identified Himself with us to redeem us from sin, so we must identify with Him in His death to sin if we would be redeemed.

The Word became flesh—"a baby at a peasant-woman's breast." That's the irreverent message of the Incarnation, the scandal of the Christmas story. That's also the joy of the gospel about which the angels sang. Is this Incarnate Son of God your Savior? He wants to be and will be, if you will allow Him to be Lord of all your life. Is He the Christ who walks and talks with you? Is He the One for whom you give up self to be identified with Him as your personal Savior and Lord? Take this to the Lord in prayer.

Prayer

O God, our heavenly Father, we rejoice in the good news of Your Son. "To us a child is born; to us a son is given." We thank and praise You for Your great love and for the gift of salvation made possible through Christ's life, death, and resurrection. With the angels we sing, "Glory to God in the highest, and on earth peace, good will among men."

In such a setting as a cattle stall the Word became flesh. Born and laid in a manger in Bethlehem, the eternal God had become man that He might bear our sins, carry our sorrows, and redeem our lives. O God, may it be our glad decision to follow that Christ Child of Bethlehem, that irreverent Savior who dared to bring You down to the ordinary and routine.

We also recall that the Savior was not received hospitably by those very people who claimed to be waiting most anxiously for Him. Herod the Great saw the Messiah as a threat to His own rule. Religious leaders of the time thought Jesus was a threat to their way of life.

Father, we cannot view these people as different from ourselves. Too often we have felt Jesus was a threat to our own way of life, and we have rejected His teaching of complete obedience to His will. We have viewed Him with indifference, relegated Him to the archives of past history, and refused to bow in submission before Him. Forgive us, Lord.

We pray for the millions of people to whom Christmas has no meaning, because they have no knowledge of the Savior. We are thankful for those who bring the good news of Christ to those who live in darkness, never having heard Jesus' name and way of salvation. We ask the Holy Spirit to bring Your messengers a fresh sense of Your presence in their labors. May they find new joy as they tell afresh the Christmas story.

May the peace and joy of Christ fill our family celebrations this year. Give us the opportunity to share His story with others. In Jesus' name we pray. Amen.

Endnotes

Preface

1. Charles Wesley, "Come, Thou Long-Expected Jesus," *Hymns for the Nativity of Our Lord*, (London, William Strahan, 1745).

A) "The faithful man God remembered" – Zechariah

2. Reverend Ike was a radio evangelist who preached about riches. He died in 2007.
3. John Bright, *The Kingdom of God*, (Nashville, Abingdon Press, 1981), 57.

B) "The ordinary man in the shadows" – Joseph

4. The Pharisees were legalistically pious laity and did not anticipate the Messiah would bring a spiritual revival (as a new priesthood) to revamp their understanding of Torah living. Instead, they expected a new political kingdom that would restore their religious freedom.

5. Oswald Chambers, *My Utmost for His Highest*, Reissue Edition (Uhrichville, Ohio: Barbour Books, 1963), 15.

C) "THE PEASANT GIRL BEHIND THE CREED" – MARY

6. The Apostles' Creed, *The Methodist Hymnal*, (New York, The Methodist Publishing House, 1939).

7. Dorothy Sayers, *Creed or Chaos?* (New York, Harcourt Brace & Co, 1949), [page].

8. E. Stanley Jones, quoted in William Barclay, *The Gospel According to Luke* (Philadelphia, Westminster Press, 1975), 19.

D) "THE IRREVERENT WORD MADE FLESH" – JESUS

9. C.S. Lewis, Introduction to J.B. Phillips' *Letters to Young Churches*, (New York: Macmillan Company, 1958), vi–vii.

10. The Council of Chalcedon in AD 451, The Creed: Incarnation of Christ. https://thewestminsterstandard.org/the-chalcedonian-creed/

11. Dorothy Sayers, *Creed or Chaos?* (New York, Harcourt Brace & Co, 1949), 5.

12. William Barclay, *The Gospel of John, Volume 1,* (Louisville: Westminster John Knox Press, 2001), 46.

13. Charles Wesley, "Glory Be to God on High," *Hymns for the Nativity of Our Lord,* (London, William Strahan, 1745).

14. Joseph Mohr, "Silent Night! Holy Night!" translated into English by John Freeman Young, *Great Hymns of the Church,* (New York: James Pott & Co, 1887).

15. A.W. Tozer, *The Pursuit of God,* (Camp Hill, Pa.: Christian Publications, Inc., 1993), 121.

16. Cleavant Derricks, Rosie Wallace, Robert C. Guidry, E.L. Jefe, "Just a Little Talk with Jesus," (Brentwood-Benson Music Publishing, Inc., 1965).

17. Norman Grubb, *Rees Howells, Intercessor,* (Fort Washington, Pa.: CLC Publications, 2016).

18. James L. Nicholson, "Lord Jesus, I Long to Be Perfectly Whole" ("Whiter Than Snow"), *Favorite Hymns,* (Chicago: Hall & McCreary, 1938), 25.

19. A. T. Kraabel, J. Andrew Overman, Robert S. MacLennan, "God-fearers," *Diaspora Jews and Judaism: Essays in Honor of, and in Dialogue with, A. Thomas Kraabel* (Republic of Moldova, Scholars Press, 1992).

ACKNOWLEDGEMENTS

W e thank first our Heavenly Father for the gift of His Son Jesus Christ, our Redeemer.

During this Advent season we are drawn to think of family and how we celebrate Christmas. First as children and then as parents and grandparents. We grew up in homes that honored the Christ child as the center of all our Christmas joy and presents under the tree. We are blessed.

The members of World Gospel Church, Terre Haute, Indiana, first heard these Advent messages, and then the cassette tapes traveled to friends and family. The sermon on Joseph is a favorite of one long-time friend and we're thankful for her encouragement for this project.

In the decision about someone to write the foreword, we chose our son, Bill, Jr. He has listened to most of his father's messages on tape or CD, sent from WGC. Bill, Jr. is a pastor with the Church of the Nazarene. Like Zechariah, he has been faithful to his calling. Thanks.

Because some aspects of book presentation are difficult, we are indebted to Erin Bartels for her professional help with title and back cover copy. And to the EABooks Publishing staff, we again extend our appreciation for their diligence during this project through all the publishing steps. Those include Cheri Cowell, James Watkins, Rebecca Ford, Robin Black, Jeanette Littleton, and Dave O'Connell (artist).

May God suit a blessing to your needs.

—Pastor Bill and Ann Coker

About the Author

Ann & Bill Coker – 50th Anniversary

A native of New Orleans, Dr. William B. Coker Sr. graduated from Tulane University in 1957. Answering the call to preach, Bill pastored churches in Louisiana, Mississippi, Kentucky, and Indiana. Bill finished graduate programs at Asbury Theological Seminary (B.D. and Th.M.) and Hebrew Union College (Ph.D.). He served as assistant professor at ATS and professor of Bible and Greek at Asbury College (University), along with two terms as Vice President of Academic Affairs. Bill was Vice President for Mission Advancement at OMS International for two years. He was senior pastor of World Gospel Church, Terre Haute, Indiana (1989–2008). Then Bill assisted the senior pastor of Free Life Community (Wesleyan) Church. He worked on many teams with the El Shaddai Emmaus community. Bill has published two books, *Words of Endearment: the Ten Commandments as a Revelation of God's Love* and *Prayers for the People: from the Heart of a Pastor.* They are available on amazon.com or from Ann. Email: al2.coker@gmail.com

Bill and his wife, Ann, now live in Indianapolis, Indiana, where they attend Southport Presbyterian Church. They have four grown children, ten grandchildren, and twelve great-grandchildren. Ann graduated from Asbury College 20 years after completing high school. She was managing editor of *Good News* magazine, and contributed to *The Woman's Study Bible*, NKJV, Thomas Nelson Publishers. She has an active blog (www.abcoker. blog), and has served several pro-life agencies. Ann is a member of Heartland Christian Writers.

Printed in Great Britain
by Amazon

27131305R00051